Use Podio

THOMAS ECCLESTONE

ISBN: 1502354950
ISBN-13: 978-1502354952

NONFICTION BOOKS BY AUTHOR

Celestia 1.6 Beginners Guide
Use LibreOffice Writer: A Beginners Guide
Use LibreOffice Impress:A Beginners Guide
Use Podio: To Manage A Small Company

CONTENTS

DEDICATION

This book is dedicated to Mr Kesterton for all his help and
support over the years.

1 GETTING TO KNOW PODIO

Why use Podio?

Podio is a sophisticated set of tools that can support all business areas in a small to medium sized company cost effectively, which can interface directly with customers and clients, and which provides a huge amount of functionality right out of the box.

Functionality that can be modified to suit your unique business needs.

This book will provide everything you need to get started with Podio. It has chapters on creating a project management system, a sales and lead system, customising Podio, and a company intranet. You can use what you learn here to use other app packs for human resources, property management and a whole host of other functional areas.

Signing up for Podio

It's easy to sign up for a free trial of Podio. Simply go to

🔒 https://podio.com in your web browser.

You'll see a box which asks you to enter your email. Do so, then

click on sign up for free

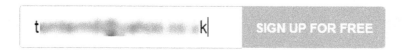

When you click on sign up for free you'll see a confirmation page:

You have mail.

We've sent your confirmation email to ~~███████████~~.

If you haven't received the email, check your junk/spam folder or send the confirmation email again. If it was sent to the wrong address, click back in your browser and enter a different one.

This page tells you to go to your email and click on the confirmation link. Go to your email program, open the email from

Podio <noreply@podio.com> and click on **Yes, it's me!** in the email.

You'll be taken to a web page that allows you to enter your name and create a password:

Your full name *

Thomas Ecclestone

Create a password *

....

Fair

By continuing, I confirm I have read and accept the Terms of Service   Next

Enter the information it requests, read the terms of service if you are concerned, and then click Next.

Podio might take a short while to set up your account, in which case you'll see:

Just one moment.

We are setting up your Podio and it will be ready in a moment.

Once it's completed you can give Podio some information about yourself. Enter who you work for

I work at:

Name of your awesome company

And what they do:

My team works on:

Client Projects, Design… It will show as your first workspace name

This field is more important, since it will show as a workspace. A workspace is used in Podio to show information or work related to one project. In the above page I chose to use "Turning's Brain" and

"Publishing" but you can use the name of your company and the main business of your company on this page.

Don't worry! You can add workspaces or change your mind later on.

Another important box is the next one, where you are able to select team members. You can think of team members as employees of the company, or people who will be able to look at (some) of the data that you enter into Podio.

At this stage I suggest that you leave these boxes blank, adding in team members later when you've set up the project to your satisfaction.

Once you're happy with your choices click

on   .

You'll see some basic information on Items. Once you've read it, click on next. Then you'll see some information on apps. Continue on to add an item.

Your First Project – The Demo

The first thing that Podio does is have you create a new project. A project may be as simple as designing a new product, or as complicated as an entire business function!

Projects are at the core of Podio as a project management application.

When looking at the screen one thing to notice is that there is a flashing green circle  by the field that you must enter next. For example it starts on Title. Once you've entered the title you want, e.g.:

Title   Write Use Podio

You'll see the circle move to the next field

Deadline   Add Deadline

When you click in the Deadline field, you'll see a calendar appear.

Deadline | Date | HH:MM

September 2014						
Su	**Mo**	**Tu**	**We**	**Th**	**Fr**	**Sa**
	1	2	3	4	5	6
7	8	9	10	11	12	13
14	15	16	17	18	19	20
21	22	23	24	25	26	27
28	29	30				

Responsible

Files

Tags

At the top of the calendar is a month field

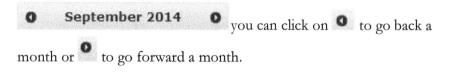 you can click on ⓞ to go back a month or ⓞ to go forward a month.

Click on one of the numbers to set the date:

	1	2	3	4	5	6
7	8	9	10	11	12	13
14	15	16	17	18	19	20
21	22	23	24	25	26	27
28	29	30				

Remember, you can change your mind later. Most companies find that deadline dates change over time. Your chosen date will be added to the field

You can chose to click on the next field if you don't want to add a specific time to the date.

When you click on Responsible you'll see a list of team members. The person you select as responsible at this stage is the Project Manager. Click on the person in the list that you want.

You'll also see a list of workspaces. Pick out the correct workspace – in practice since you've only created one it'll be whatever area you chose during installation!

The next option allows you to add a file:

Files   Choose a file

Click on choose a file to show an add file dialogue.

My computer   Select files from your computer

Add file service   Choose files

Connect your favorite
online services

Drag 'n drop files here

Cancel   Done

You can drag files into the Drag n' Drop box, or click on

Choose files
to open a dialogue.

Files added at this point might be requirement documents, terms of reference, or any other document that is relevant to the project.

Once you're happy that you've added all the files that you want, click on tags

Tags   Add tags

You can add whatever tags relate to your project. When you've got a large number of projects tags can be useful to find the particular project that you are working on.

Check through all the information you've added. When you're happy click on ![Save Project].

Modify a template

While you've created a basic project using Podio sometimes the basic information that you add at this stage isn't enough. You can change the template that Podio provides for a project by clicking Modify Template.

Once you do this, the Modify template screen will appear:

This is divided into a set of Fields options (1) and the fields you've actually got in your current template.

If you click and hold on Text, then move it across to the space between title and deadline then let go you'll add a new text field to the template:

A ·   Title

A   Text

□ ·   Deadline

Once you let go the field will appear where you dropped it:

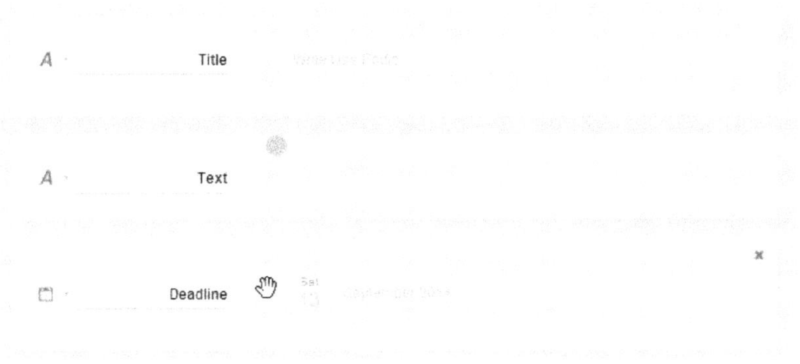

A ·   Title

A ·   Text

□ ·   Deadline

You can rename a text by clicking on the underlined section on the right,

A ·   Text

And typing the title of the field. In this case, 'Description'.

A ·   Description

Once you've finished modifying the Template, you can click on **Done** . Note that I'll go into more detail on changing templates later.

Once you've clicked on done you'll see the new field appear in

the project information:

You can add in the description by clicking in the box provided. You'll see a text editing box appear which has normal formatting features such as bold, italic underline and so on

Plus undo and redo .

Enter in your Description:

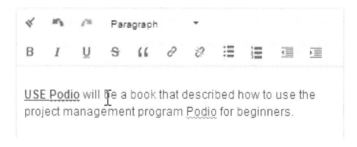

One thing that many people are interested in is accountability. Podio stores an activity log of what people have done in a project. You can see this activity log in the right hand corner of the screen:

Now that you've finished the initial demo, look at the right hand corner where it says

And click on:

Congratulations, you've finished the initial demo!

Adding a New Task

If your project was making a cup of coffee, tasks might include buying the ingredients, cleaning the cup and boiling the coffee. You can think of a task as a part of a project with measurable outcomes that you assign to a specific person.

It's easy to add a new task in Podio. In the Project page, click on

Add Task:

This displays the New Task dialogue.

Give the task a name by typing into the Enter a task box:

For example, in our project Write USE Podio, a task might be to write Chapter One

Assign someone to be responsible for the task by either typing an email address or clicking on the Pick a Contact box

People outside of Podio

Note that you can assign a task to someone outside Podio by clicking on:

Which opens up contact dialogue. Either type a name into the search to find the contact you want to add:

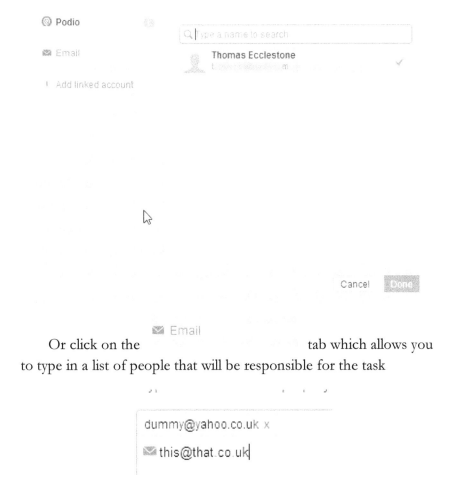

Or click on the ✉ Email tab which allows you to type in a list of people that will be responsible for the task

You can click the × to remove an email from the list, and once you're happy click **Done** . This will return you to the add task dialogue.

Setting due date and time

In the same way that you can set a due date and time for a Project you can also set a due date and time for a task. Click on the No Due Date to set the due date:

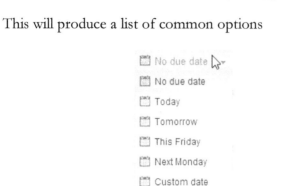

This will produce a list of common options

You can select Custom Date to choose a date that isn't on the list.

Type a description of the task into

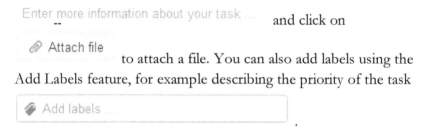

and click on

Attach file to attach a file. You can also add labels using the Add Labels feature, for example describing the priority of the task

.

One feature that some people find very useful is the Remind me option. Click on to produce a list of options of when to remind yourself about a task. This will send an email to you on the due date, or a specified amount of time before (including the previous day).

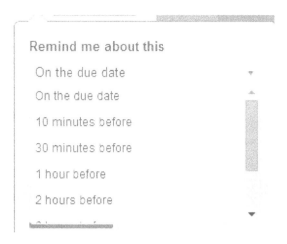

Once you're happy with the task that you've created

click  .

Viewing the Calendar

Once you've created tasks it can be very useful to see them displayed on a calendar. This allows you to plan your week ahead of schedule and see when assignments may clash or there may be other problems.

At the top of the screen, you'll find the Podio taskbar:

Click on the Calendar icon to open up your calendar

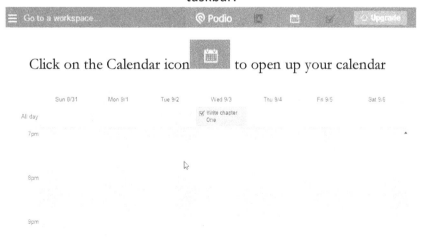

By default this starts by showing weeks, but on the right hand side you can select months or days:

Month   Week   Day

If you click and hold on a task and drag it to a different day or a different time in the day, the deadline for the task will change. When you have many different tasks all due at different times this ability is a life saver

One thing that people often don't notice is the show icon. If you click on ✦ the you can restrict the tasks that Podio shows to one of the following options:

> **Show:**
> ⦿ Everything date-related in all the workspaces I'm a member of
> ◯ I'm following (e.g., everything I've been referenced on, interacted with or manually chosen to follow)
> ◯ Involving and related to me (e.g., meetings I'm invited to and app items I'm referenced on in a Contact field)
> ◯ Directly involving me (e.g., meetings I'm invited to and tasks assigned to me)

Viewing the activity stream

Sometimes you may wish to view a log of all the things that have happened in Podio. To do so click on the Podio logo in the Podio taskbar.

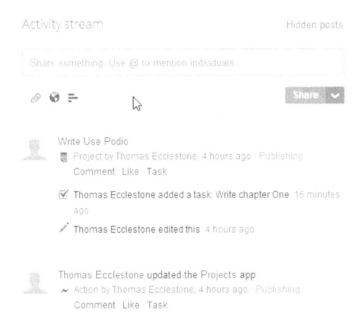

I'll go into some more detail about this view later; you can use it to add notes, address a particular person, and share files, internet links and other information that people need to know.

Adding Employees

To add employees to your workspaces, click on the contacts list . On the right hand side click on + ADD MEMBER . .

As a rule I suggest adding an employee to the Employee Network first:

Choose a workspace to add these members to:

Employee Network ▼

And clicking on Next .

In the next screen, you'll see a contacts dialogue. Since a new employee hasn't been added to the company yet, I suggest typing in the employees email address:

When you've added all the emails, click

on  .

The next screen will confirm that you've sent an invitation to your employee:

His email address will receive an invitation. Once he clicks

on [Go to Podio] he'll be taken to the employee network.

Next Chapter

In this chapter we've discussed some basic Project Management capabilities in Podio. But we've only really touched the very tip of the surface of what you can do with Podio:

- Creating basic projects
- Assigning tasks
- Looking at them in a calendar

In the next chapter I'm going to give some more information on the Project Collaboration Workspace which allows you to manage projects with far more control.

2 THE PROJECT COLLABORATION WORKSPACE

In this chapter I'll describe how to add and use a Project Collaboration workspace. This is a standard workspace designed to allow you to create and manage Projects, Deliverables, assign roles to team members and manage project meetings.

While Podio allows you a great deal of flexibility, these standard workspaces are often a very good place to start when tackling standard problems. As you get more familiar with Podio you can then modify them to be closer to your particular requirements.

Modifying your Profile

You can modify your profile by clicking on and then Complete your profile . You'll see a page appear with an activity log on the left, and your profile on the right.

Fill out the fields such as name, title, click on **Choose image** to upload your profile picture and so on.

Remember that this is a public profile so don't include anything that you don't want fellow employees to know!

Click **Done** when you're happy with your profile.

Workspaces, Apps and Items

An App is almost like a program that you add to Podio that contains information that and functionality that is related to a particular task. An Item is one instance of an app – i.e. a particular sales record say, or a staff meeting on the 11th September.

Apps are combined together into workspaces. A workspace is somewhere that combines all the functionality you need to do a particular type of task.

For example, you might create a workspace to deal with project management. In fact, that's just what we're doing in this chapter.

Adding a workspace

Click on the Workspace options icon at the top left hand corner

of the screen ▆. At the top of the workspace options you'll see three workspaces: Employee Network, a Demo Workspace, and the workspace you created during Chapter One (Publishing, in my case).

To add a workspace, click

on ＋ Create a workspace ⌐.

Podio has some standard workspaces that provide things that most companies use, such as Project Collaboration, Lead Management, and a company Intranet. You can also create an empty workspace which you will customise from the start.

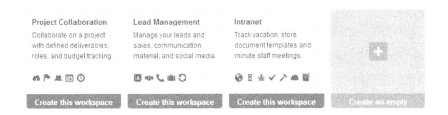

Project Collaboration Workspace

If you want to create a workspace for a particular project click on **Project Collaboration** .

You can enter a project name into the first box:

What do you want to call your workspace?

Project Collaboration

And then chose your Access settings. For example, you may want to limit access on some projects to invitation only, or you may want every employee to join a particular project.

Access settings ⑦

◉   Open - visible and open for all employees to join

    ⌕ Automatically join new employees

○   Private - invite only

Once you've chosen your options click on **Create & Invite** and a new dialogue showing which employees to add to your project will appear.

You can either type email addresses into the box:

Or click on the contacts icon,   which displays a list of people to add:

When you click on a name to select it a tick icon appears   .
Clicking on the name a second time will deselect it. Once you're

happy with your choices, click   Done   .

Note there is one very important feature at the bottom. The
Role. This controls the access functions of individuals over the
workspace. By default it is Workspace

admin: Role : Workspace admin   , which gives a large degree of
control. In most cases you should change this by clicking on it and
then clicking on   Regular member   .

A regular member has a lot less control over the administrative
features of the workspace. This prevents them from making mistakes
that could take a lot of work to resolve.

Once you're happy, click the Add button

Add to Project Collaboration   (note that the workspace name will be
whatever you chose earlier). When you click on done a confirmation
dialogue will display.

Views in the Project Collaboration workspace.

We've already worked in a very basic Project workspace. Once

25

we add a Project Collaboration Workspace we've got access to a whole host of new apps and capabilities.

At the top of the workspace you can see six apps:

You've already met Activity and Projects. Deliverables, Roles, Timesheets and Meetings are all new. And, in fact, when you click on Projects you'll find that it is much more advanced than the example we saw in Chapter One.

It's really important to note that Podio is very highly customisable. It's possible to develop your own replacement Project app which matches how you work as a company.

Inviting an employee onto the new workspace

While the first step allows you to add employees to a workspace, over the life of a project you can always add more. At the top of the Activities apps you'll see a list of the people you've already invited onto the workspace. Click on invite to add more

Project Collaboration 2

You'll see the invite dialogue I explained earlier, and can invite the employee easily.

Deleting an employee from the workspace

The above frame in the window also allows you to delete users from the workspace. Move your mouse into the frame and you'll see a little ⚞ icon. Click on it.

A list of options will appear. At the top of the list is 👥 Manage Members ᶜ. Click on it, and you'll see the manage members dialogue.

All members of Project Collaboration   All users   ▾   🔍 Search

User		Type	Role	Actions
👤	Thomas Ecclestone tho⋯⋯⋯uk	Employee	Regular member	Actions
👤	Thomas Ecclestone ton⋯⋯om	Employee	Admin member	Actions ▾

This will show a list of members. Click on Actions, then Remove from workspace to delete a member from the workspace

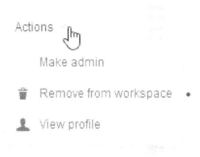

Actions 🖐

Make admin

🗑 Remove from workspace •

👤 View profile

Going to a particular workspace or returning to the Workspace view

Sometimes, when you're deep in the middle of managing a work space you may want to return to the main workspace view. For example, when you've finished adding deliverables.

At the top of the screen next to three lines there's the name of the current workspace you're working on:

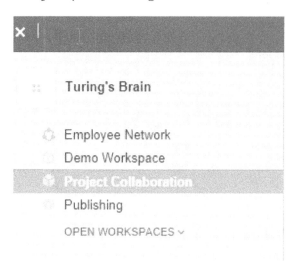

Click on it, and you'll see a list of workspaces. Click on whichever workspace you want to go to:

You'll go to that workspace's main view!

Adding a Project

This workspace isn't much use without adding a project!

Click on Projects ₀ to open the Project app. The first time you open the Project App you might get a few hints about how to use it – especially as there won't be any projects available yet.

That's because each workspace is independent of the others. When you created the Project collaboration workspace it didn't include the previous project you created. That belongs to another workspace.

To add a new project click **+ Add Project** on the right hand side of the screen.

While you've added a project in a different workspace you'll find that the template for this project app is far more comprehensive.

First, give the project a

* **Project Name**   The New Project|

name.

Then, click on   Add Project manager   to add a project manager.

You'll see a list of people you've invited into the workspace. Click on one of them

One difference between the basic project you added in chapter one and the Project Collaboration workspace is that team members can have roles. A project manager is an important role that assigns deliverables and manages tasks.

The next step is to choose your stage:

Stage   Placeholder for future project   Planning   In progress   Complete   Archived

Normally, when creating a project for the first time your stage will be Placeholder or Planning. But sometimes you may want to start a project at a later stage.

Click on the stage you want. When you chose a stage, you'll see a box around the selected stage:

Placeholder for future project

Next, click on Add Project kick-off and end dates. You'll see one set of dates and times, click on the date you want to begin.

Once you select a date, you'll end up in the HH:MM box. Either type in a time to start the project, or go to the next date box and select the date to end the project.

At this stage you can't edit the deliverables for the project, so scroll down and click on Add Definition to add a project definition

When you're finished scroll down and click on Add Targets to add information about targets, or Add Resources to add information about resources.

You can add files to the project by clicking on choose a file

Files   Choose a file

This will display a files dialogue box like the one you've already seen.

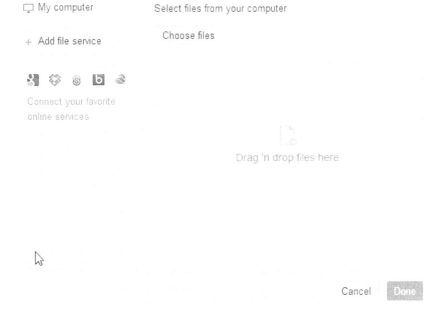

My computer   Select files from your computer

+ Add file service   Choose files

Connect your favorite
online services

Drag 'n drop files here

Cancel   Done

Again, you can drag a file over to the drag 'n drop box, or click on choose files to display an open box.

Once you've clicked Done , you can click Add tags and enter in labels that are useful for identifying the project.

While this is more complicated than the Project app in chapter one you only normally need to add a project once. Check that the information you've added for the project is correct and then click on

You've created the Project. You'll see the current project information in the window. You can edit fields and change project information if you want. Under the blue bar at the top of the screen is set of navigation links. Click on Projects to return to the main Project page:

You'll see that the new project has been created:

Of course, a project isn't much use without tasks or deliverables, so I'll describe how the Project Collaboration workspace tackles these features next!

Adding Deliverables

All projects have deliverables. Maybe they are things like a user manual, creating a requirements document, or conveyancing for a real estate transaction. A deliverable is something concrete that the project produces.

To manage the project deliverables, click on

To add a deliverable, click

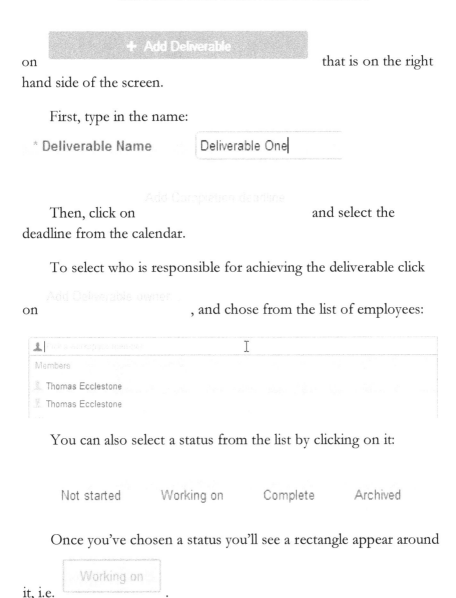

on **+ Add Deliverable** that is on the right hand side of the screen.

First, type in the name:

* Deliverable Name   Deliverable One|

Then, click on Add Completion deadline and select the deadline from the calendar.

To select who is responsible for achieving the deliverable click on Add Deliverable owner , and chose from the list of employees:

Members
Thomas Ecclestone
Thomas Ecclestone

You can also select a status from the list by clicking on it:

Not started   Working on   Complete   Archived

Once you've chosen a status you'll see a rectangle appear around it, i.e. Working on .

You can also specify how far you've gone towards achieving the deliverable using the progress chart.

Progress   0%   ×

Click and hold on the scroll bar and move right (to increase the progress) or left (to reduce it) letting go when you've given the deliverable the right completion. For many deliverables this is a subjective measure but it can still be useful to determine how far you've got before you complete the deliverable.

When we created a project we didn't provide any schedule or budget information. That's because this is controlled in the Deliverable app. It's very important to specify this when you're adding a deliverable.

Click on Add Hours allocated for this deliverable... to add the amount of time you have to work on this deliverable.

You'll be able to enter in the number of hours and minutes into the appropriate box:

Hours   Minutes   Seconds

Once you've finished editing the field it will show the data you've entered. If you change your mind you can still change the time allocated by clicking on the time

Hours allocated for this   12 hours 1 minute
deliverable

You can also control the deliverables budget by clicking on Add Budget... . By default the deliverables budget is in dollars.

Enter the budget you have for this deliverable:

Budget $ ˅   20,000.00|

You can't alter the time already spent on the deliverable directly. You have to do this via the time sheets app that I will describe later on.

To add a description of the deliverable click

on  . A text editing dialogue will be displayed.

Deliverable description

This is a **Deliverable Description**

The next field, the Project Reference, links a deliverable to the Project that it belongs to. This allows the deliverables budget and time allocation to be accurately monitored.

Click on  by Project reference. This will produce a list of projects. Click on the correct project:

Project reference

Projects

The New Project
  Project Collaboration - Turning a Brain

Create new item

You can also add files to the deliverable by clicking

on  , or add tags by clicking on .

Once you're satisfied that the information you've added is

correct, click on Save Deliverable

You can edit the deliverable you just added, or click on Deliverables on the navigation links to return to the page showing a list of project deliverables:

Project Collaboration > 🏛 **Deliverables** > Deliverable One

In the Deliverables window you'll see a list of deliverables that you're working on:

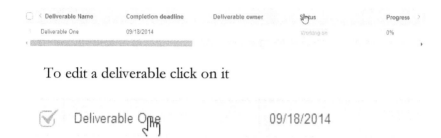

To edit a deliverable click on it

☑ Deliverable One   09/18/2014

Delete a Deliverable

In the list of deliverables hover your number over the number of the item on the list that you want to edit:

Deliverable One   09/18/2014

You'll see the number replaced by a check box ☐ Deliverable One . Check the deliverable you want to delete.

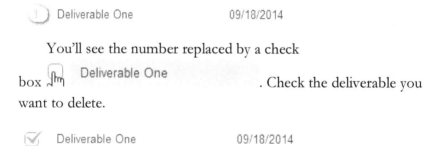

At the top right hand side of the list click the delete icon 🗑 . You'll see a warning dialogue:

Delete 1 Deliverables

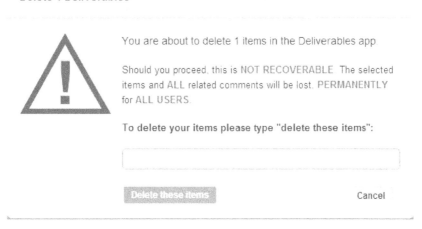

Type the required phrase (delete these items) into the box then click .

Assigning Roles to the Project

Once you've created deliverables it can be very useful to assign specific team members to roles within the project. The Roles App allows you to do this.

Click on to run the roles app. At first the Roles app will be empty. You can add a new role by clicking on .

Note that Project Manager, Deliverable and Task Owners are all specialist roles within Podio. The Roles act, however, allows you to create more specialist roles for individual projects.

First, give the role a name

Name of Role   Writer

Then click on *Add Contact* to add the people that you want to add to this role.

You'll see a list of workspace members

Click on the names from the list of the people you want to add to roles. It's important to note that a team member can take on more than one role.

To describe the role click on *Add Role description* which will bring up a text window that you can add to.

One field that you might not have to add is location. But sometimes a role is limited to a particular place. Where necessary, click *Add Location* and then type in the where it's based.

Location | I

You can add tags and files to the role. Check that everything you've added is right and click

 .

Once you've saved it, you'll still be on the role that you've just added. You can either edit it and save it again, or return to the main page of the app by clicking on the navigation links

Project Collaboration > 👥 Roles > Writer

If you go to the main app view you'll see what you've just added included in the list:

You can edit a role by clicking on it from the main list.

Deleting a role

In order to delete a role you have to be editing it. First, open the

main roles app view by clicking on 👥 Roles (if it's not visible on the page you're in, go to the Workspace view.)

In the main roles app view you'll see a list of roles. Click on the one you want to edit.

On the top of the screen there's an actions button. Click it to see a list of actions

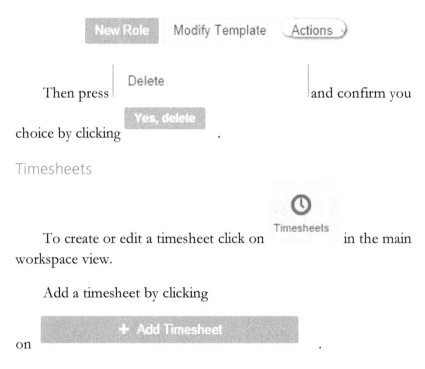

Then press Delete and confirm you choice by clicking Yes, delete .

Timesheets

To create or edit a timesheet click on Timesheets in the main workspace view.

Add a timesheet by clicking

on + Add Timesheet .

NOTE: A timesheet is related to a particular project deliverable. If you are working on more than one deliverable on a particular day create two timesheets.

Add a title to the timesheet by entering it into the box provided:

* Title   Wrote Chapter One

This title should be as meaningful as possible – for example including the name of the deliverable.

To specify who did the work click on Add Employee and select from the list:

Employee

Members

   Thomas Ecclestone

   Thomas Ecclestone

Workspaces

   Project Collaboration (2)

     Turing's Brain

Click on Add Date. to add the day you worked from and to using the provided calendar. You use this the same way you entered the date for the deliverable or project deadlines

You must specify how long you worked on the timesheet. To do this click on *Add Time spent* .which will bring up time fields:

| | Hours | | Minutes | | Seconds |

Once you've finished editing the time will appear next to the "time spent" field. You can click on the time (highlighted below) to edit it again

Time spent   2 hours 10 minutes

Finally click on Hourly rate to specify the cost of the time *Add Hourly rate* and put in the cost per hour:

* Hourly rate $ ∨ [   ]

You must link a timesheet to a deliverable. Scroll down to Deliverable worked on and click on *Type to search for items* .

You'll see a list of deliverables. Click the appropriate deliverable:

Deliverable worked on

Deliverables

Deliverable One
Project Collaboration - Turing's Brain

Create new item

When you click

Add Any problems or requests   or   Add Details of work   you get a text
box to enter this information. You can also add a file by clicking

Choose a file
      or add tags   Add tags   .

Once you're happy with your timesheet click

Save Timesheet

.

Note that once you save it some of the automated fields such as
total cost are updated:

Total cost   21.67 USD   . This has an effect on both
project and deliverable budgets so be careful.

On saving a timesheet, you'll remain with that timesheet open.
This allows you to continue editing the timesheet.

Actions ˅

To print the timesheet that you're editing, click on
and then click on Print from the list of options.

If you click on Delete from the above list you'll get a dialogue asking you to confirm if you want to delete the timesheet. Click

Yes, delete to delete it.

Once you've finished editing the timesheet either click

New Timesheet on the top left hand side of the screen to create a new timesheet, or return to the timesheet app main view by clicking Timesheets in the navigation links:

Project Collaboration > ⏱ Timesheets > Write Chapter ONe

When you return to the main view you'll see the timesheet you just made appear in a list of timesheets:

To delete timesheet(s) from the main timesheet app view

In the main timesheet list, hover your mouse over the number of the timesheet you want to delete

	Title	Employee	Date
	Write Chapter One	Thomas Ecclestone	09/04/2014

Until it changes to a square

box ⬜ Write Chapter One . Click on the box to select

the timesheet.

☑ Write Chapter One   Thomas Ecclestone . If

you change your mind, click on ☑ by a timesheet to deselect it.
You can scroll down the list until you've selected all the timesheets
you want to delete.

Click on 🗑 to delete the selected timesheets.

A warning dialogue will appear

Delete 1 Timesheets

⚠ You are about to delete 1 items in the Timesheets app.

Should you proceed, this is NOT RECOVERABLE. The selected
items and ALL related comments will be lost, PERMANENTLY
for ALL USERS.

To delete your items please type "delete these items":

[   ]

[Delete these items]   Cancel

Enter the text that it asks you to enter in the box, then

press [Delete these items] .

Meetings

You can manage your meetings using the meetings app. In the main workspace view click

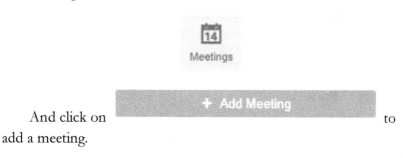

And click on  to add a meeting.

First, enter a title that describes the reason for the meeting

* **Meeting Title** | Enter a title

Add a date by clicking on Add Date... and selecting it from the calendar.

There's a list of attendees at the meeting next. The person who creates a meeting is included automatically but you can edit it by

clicking on Add / Remove participants .

Adding people to the meeting is easy, just click on them in the list:

If you want to remove someone from the meeting it's easy. By each person's name is a little cross.  If you click it, they're removed from the list.

To specify the agenda click Add Agenda , to add minutes after the meeting click Add Minutes/Notes and to specify the location for the meeting click Add Location .

Once you're happy click Save Meeting . All participants to the meeting will be notified by email.

You can print the meeting by clicking on Actions ˅ and then selecting print from the options:

Actions ˅

Print

You can delete it by selecting Delete from Actions ˅ and then hitting Yes, delete .

Clicking **New Meeting** will create a new meeting, or clicking meetings in the navigation links will return you to the main meetings view Project Collaboration > 🖼 Meetings > Enter a title .

In the main meeting app view you'll see the meeting appear in the list of meetings. Clicking on it will open it so you can edit it or delete it. You'll often edit a meeting after the event to add your meeting minutes to it.

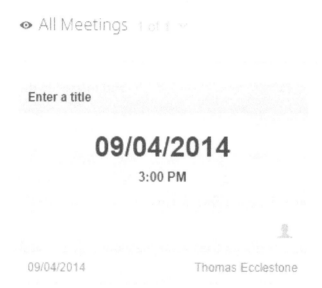

👁 All Meetings 1 of 1

Enter a title

09/04/2014

3:00 PM

09/04/2014   Thomas Ecclestone

App Tasks

One thing that I haven't mentioned so far is that each app has another facility that allows you to create tasks that are related to that app. So, for example, in the Project app you could create a task to create a new project, or in the deliverable app you can create a task to edit a deliverable.

You can see the tasks for an app on the right had side:

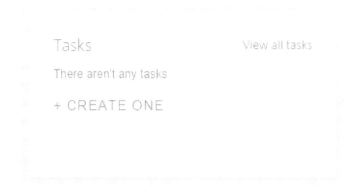

To create a task, click on + CREATE ONE . A new task dialogue will appear, with the app type at the top e.g. **New task on Roles**. First click on ☑ Enter a task ... and put in a descriptive name for the task. For example@

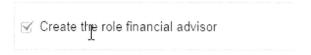

Then click on |Pick a contact or type an email address and select a person who is responsible for the task from the list of names. You can add more than one person if necessary.

> ⊥ Pick a contact or type an email address
> People
> ⊥ Thomas Ecclestone
> ⊥ Thomas Ecclestone
> Workspaces

Click on 📅 No due date ▼ to add a due date from the list (custom date gives you a calendar to pick a date from)

No due date ▾

No due date

Today

Tomorrow

Next Monday

Custom date

Click on ⊙ --:-- to set a due by time, and

🔓 Shared ▾ to specify if it is shared (i.e. visible to everyone on the workspace) or private (visible to people with admin privileges and also to the people who have been assigned the task).

You can add text information about the task

using *i* Enter more information about your task ... , and like normal can also add a file and labels.

If you want to be reminded about the task click on 🐻 , which allows you to select a reminder date or time from a list of options. Once you're happy with the information you've added, click

Create task .

The new task will appear in the tasks section of the page.

Tasks ▷ View all tasks

☐ Create the role financial advisor
Thomas Ecclestone

Click on ⬚View all tasks to look at all tasks in that app, and click on the ⬚ by a task to show that you've completed it.

☑ ~~Create the role financial advisor~~
~~Thomas Ecclestone~~

Next Chapter

In this chapter I've described a standard workspace called Project Collaboration that can be very useful when you want to manage projects. But Podio is far more powerful than that.

Many companies will want CRM functionality to manage the Sales and lead pipeline. Podio provides a pack of applications that can provide this functionality for most small and medium businesses. The next chapter will show you this pack in action.

3 SALES AND LEAD MANAGEMENT

In this chapter I'll give you a brief introduction to the app market, and then describe an app package that allows you to add sales and lean management to your workspace.

Podio is a highly extensible and customisable workflow tool. There are dozens of apps that you can add to it which allow it to do all sorts of things from classroom management to property management. While it's outside the scope of this book to describe all of these app packages, most companies are going to require sales and lead management tools and Podio has a rich premade package that can tackle most companies requirements.

Creating an empty workspace

In chapter two while creating a workspace you were given a choice of three common packages. Once you've made this initial workspace the process for creating a new one is slightly different. It's best to start from an empty workspace.

First click on . And then

+ Create a workspace

.

Enter a name for the workspace

What do you want to call your workspace?

Sales Management

Choose whether to make the workspace open or private.

- ◉ Open - visible and open for all employees to join
    - ☐ Automatically join new employees
- ○ Private - invite only

This works in the same way as the last example. You can also toggle the option to automatically join new employees.

Once you're happy click Create & Invite .

An add persons dialogue appears. You can change the role of the people you are adding by clicking

on Role : Workspace admin and add people using the Pick People box:

In the same way as you did in the prior step. Alternatively, bring

up a contacts dialogue by clicking on which allows you to add people from your contacts list or a list of email addresses.

Remember that you can invite people at a later stage and so you'd normally only invite the people who will be involved in setting up the workspace while creating a new work space.

Once you're happy with your selections click

to **Add to Sales Management** .

You'll see a confirmation dialogue. To close it hit **Done** .

What you've created doesn't look the same as your previous workspace. It is very much an empty workspace without much functionality at all.

Don't worry about this. We're about to add some functionality!

The Podio App Market

Click on **ADD APP** to add functionality to your empty workspace.

You've got the choice to create your own app, or you can use apps that other people have created. We're going to add an app package called Sales and Lead Management to Podio. To do this you have to go to the App market because it is a set of apps that other people have already designed for you.

To go to the app market click on **Go to the App Market** .

You'll notice that the screen is divided into two areas, the Functional areas which reflect different business areas that Podio has applications or packs for

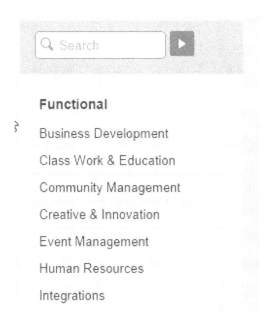

On the right hand side there is the App market itself. This is divided into packs, which are groups of applications that reflect one business area:

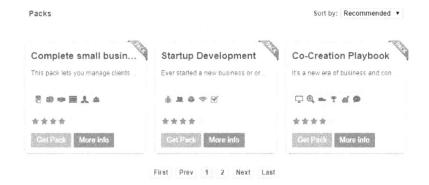

And below them are individual apps:

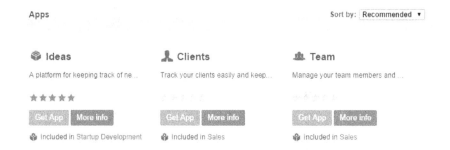

Of course both these screen shots will change depending what functional area you're working with at the moment.

Since in this chapter we're going to use a basic pack to develop a sales and lead management system, the first step is to go to the Sales & CRM functional business area by scrolling down until the penultimate item on the Functional list on the left hand side of the screen and clicking on

Sales & CRM

You'll see that the pack section of the app market changes to include a number of different packs. Each pack is related to the functional area you just selected.

Most functional areas have a lot of packs. Below the packs there are numbers you click to see more options:

If you can't find the app that you need easily, you can search for it using a search box at the top left hand of the screen.

The first Pack that we're going to include is called Lead Management. Thumb through the numbers until you get to it:

Click on  .

Once you've chosen to add the pack a little progress dialogue will appear with the title **Install app or pack** . You may find that it takes some time before you can install the pack.

Select your workspace in the install pack dialogue:

Once Podio has finished installing the pack you'll see a new dialogue:

Which confirms that you've installed the package.

Click on  .

You'll be in the main workspace view. Note that you've got a lot of new apps: Leads, Sales, Communications etc.

While each pack is pretty comprehensive you may want to add even more capabilities to your workspace. For example, the above sales management workspace doesn't have the ability to store sales scripts.

Go back to the App Market by clicking 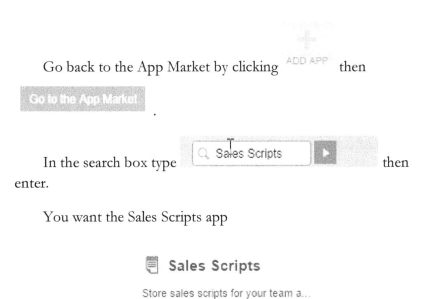 then

Go to the App Market .

In the search box type [Sales Scripts] then enter.

You want the Sales Scripts app

🖺 **Sales Scripts**

Store sales scripts for your team a...

★ ★ ★ ★ ★

Get App   More info

Hit Get App to get the app.

Choose your workspace in the

dialogue  Sales Management ▾ and click Next .

You'll see an App Installed icon:

App installed   ✕

App added to Sales Management

🖺

Try app now   Close

Click on Try app now to see the new app in your workspace:

It's really not possible to describe each pack or app in this book but you can find out more information on each pack before you use it with **More info** .

Products

To keep a record of what products you're selling click on the

Products app in the main workspace view.

Then click on **+ Add Product** to add a product.

You can add a product name **Product Name** [   ] ,

A new product owner *Add Product owner...* which brings up a list of employees.

You can also *Add Price...* and *Add Possible discounts...* which inform the sales team of the possible discounts and price terms that are available.

There are product statuses (whether the product exists)

Product idea   Currently developing it   Sales ready

You can also add a description, files *Choose a file* or tags. If you've got an advert like a poster, or a picture of the packaging you

can add it using   Add image   . This brings up a file dialogue.

Modifying the App template

At this stage you might be wondering if there's a way to extend the app so that it can contain, for example, a variable pricing structure (i.e. if you were licensing software you might want to have a different price per unit for 1-10 product licenses compared to a site license for more than 10 products).

At the top left hand side is a button   Modify Template   . Click it and you get the App modification window.

On the left hand side is a list of different fields that you can use:

Fields

A   Text

≡   Category

📅   Date

⚚   Relationship

👤   Contact

123   Number

🔗   Link

🖼   Image

💱   Money

%   Progress

🖥   Calculation

And on the right hand side is a list of the fields you're already including in the App.

In this list, click on Price

Hit the ✖ on the right hand side of the field.

You'll see the remove field dialogue. Toggle

☐ Also remove field from existing app items on if you want to remove this field from all existing app items. We've already dealt with app items; if we add a new product that is an app item. Since you haven't already used the app there aren't any existing app items but if you were to delete a field in an app that's been in use for a while you'd probably chose to toggle this item on.

If you're happy click **Yes, delete** . Podio may sometimes ask you to confirm this decision.

In the list of fields, put your mouse over Text, hold your left mouse button down and drag the box between Product Owner and Possible discounts.

Then let go. A text field will appear after Product owner. Double click on Text

Type in the name of the field (in this case, Price)

You may also want to add another status to the Product. Scroll down to the Status field

And type in your new status

Sales Ended|

then

press enter.

You can add several other types of field. Once you're happy with your changes, click Done . This will make your changes go live.

Note that the changes you've made to the template will have immediate effect on the Product App.

Any future products you add will have the same basic template you've just created.

Sales Scripts

Sales scripts are useful when giving presentations, receiving calls or otherwise interacting with customers. You can use the script to make sure that everyone remains on message. Podio provides a basic sales script app that you can customise if necessary to match your work flow using the methods outlined above.

From the main workspace view click on Sales Scripts to open the sales scripts app.

Click on + Add Sales Script to add a new sales script.

You can add a
title,

* Title		

and also Add Cases for use... to specify when you'll use the script.

Click on Add Script... to include the full script. You can select the owner of the script by clicking Add Responsible for updating ... and selecting them from the drop down list:

Responsible for updating

Members
Thomas Ecclestone
Thomas Ecclestone
Workspaces
Sales Management (2)
Turing's Brain

It's also possible to add a file or tags to the script.

Press **Save Sales Script** to save the script.

Like all Podio apps you can print it from the Action button

Actions
Print

Once you've saved it, click on Sales Scripts in the navigation window to return to the main sales app:

Sales Management > Sales Scripts > Books Sales Script

You'll see the new script appear in the app view.

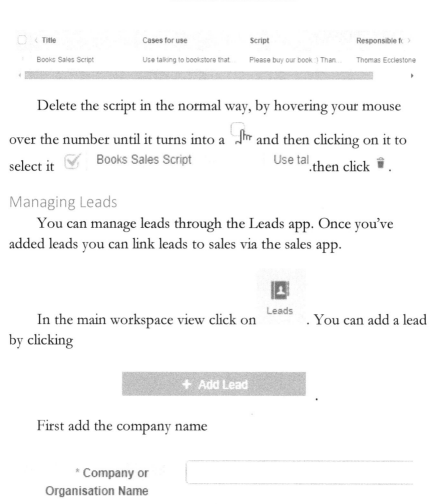

Delete the script in the normal way, by hovering your mouse over the number until it turns into a ⌐╨ and then clicking on it to select it ☑ Books Sales Script   Use tal.then click 🗑 .

Managing Leads

You can manage leads through the Leads app. Once you've added leads you can link leads to sales via the sales app.

In the main workspace view click on   . You can add a lead by clicking

First add the company name

The next thing is to Add Lead contacts... this works a little differently to most of the other fields that we've added. You see a list of existing contacts open up. Since you haven't added any yet, this will be empty. Click on Add new contact (assuming the contact you want to add isn't in the list):

You can add the contact in the next dialogue including name, title, organization, and phone and email address and photo if one is available

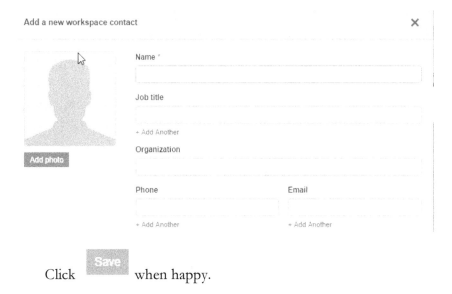

Click Save when happy.

Note that when you save it the contact is added to the contacts field, but when you create a new lead in the future it will also be displayed in the pick a contact field.

You can say who is responsible for contacting the lead by clicking on *Add Lead owner...* and choosing from the list of names.

Add Expected total value of lead... allows you to enter an amount of money you expect to make from the lead. This is obviously an important field as it allows you to prioritise certain high value leads over less valuable leads.

Equally, there's a slider that allows you to say how likely the lead owner considers that the expected value will be realised.

Probability of projected
possible value

The status field allows you to set certain statuses for the lead:

Qualified lead   Cold lead   Contacted   In dialogue   Sale   Followed up for sale

Second sale   Further sales

Remember that it's possible to add or remove statuses in this field by modifying the app template with the Modify Template button.

The Add Next follow-up... sets a date by which time the lead owner must ensure that the lead has been followed up. It's possible to create a report based on this information so that every day you can see urgent leads.

The next fields are address fields

Street address   Add Street address...

City   Add City...

State/County/Province   Add State/County/Province...

Zip code/Post code   Add Zip code/Post code...

Country   Add Country...

But there's one field that you haven't seen before. The address field:

Add Office address map...   . Click on it, and you can enter your post code or zip code (or, in the UK, the first half of your postcode) and it lists the location:

Click on the location address. You'll see a map of that location

Like most apps you can also add files and tags if necessary, and save it by clicking [Save Lead ⌄] You can print or delete it using Actions ⌄ , continue editing the lead or click on [New Lead] or leads in the navigation links

 to get back to the main leads app view.

A list of leads will be displayed.

○ All Leads 1 of 1 ⌄			⌄ AZ ✕ ▥ Save view Actions ⌄	
☐ ‹ Company or Organisati...	Lead contacts	Lead owner	Expected total value of le...	Probabilit ›
⋮ Turing's Brain	Thomas Ecclestone	Thomas Ecclestone	USD 1,000.00	18%

We'll see that there is a link between the sales app and the leads app. When you make a sale, the values of the following fields will be updated automatically:

Current value of sales
made to this lead

Average value of sales
made to this lead

Making Sales

While we've just discussed managing leads Podio also has the ability to manage sales. You shouldn't try to manage a sale until you've created a lead for it in the leads app.

Once you want to record a sale, click 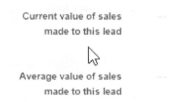 in the main workspace view.

You can add a sale by clicking

on ＋ Add Sale .

The Sales app included in the Lead Management pack is relatively basic. People do often make adjustments to it in order to match their company workflow. We'll describe how to make these adjustments later on in the book. This chapter will just describe the vanilla version.

First enter the organisation name,

* Customer
Organisation/Company Name   Turing's Brain

And then the sale status

Sale in progress   Sale closed   Invoice sent

When you click on Add Person in charge of sale... it provides you with a list of employees. 7

It's possible to enter the probable value of the sale

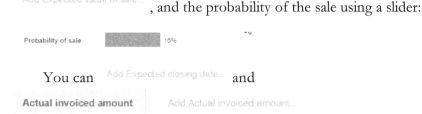, and the probability of the sale using a slider:

You can *Add Expected closing date...* and

Actual invoiced amount Add Actual invoiced amount...

There are two linking fields. A linking field is one where you link to the items in another app. One of them. When you click

Type to search for items you'll see a list of the products that you added in the product app:

You can click create new item to create a product if you haven't already created the one that you're selling.

Once you've added a product you'll see displayed in the field:

There are two linking fields.

Leads (Type to search for items) is the second linking field. Clicking it will produce a list of leads:

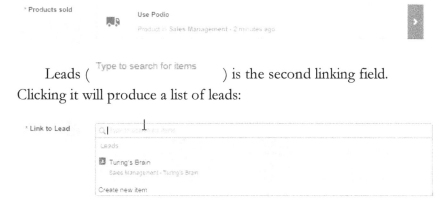

You can create a new lead by clicking create new item, or click on an existing lead.

At a minimum people often decide to modify the sales template to include contracts, delivery deadlines, and similar nonstandard terms. But I'll show you how to do this later on.

Press **Save Sale** to save the changes you've made. You can delete or print using the Actions button, make a new sale by clicking on **New Sale**, or navigate to the main sale app view by clicking on sales in the navigation links Sales Management ⟩ ■ Sales ⟩ Turing's Brain .

Once you're in the Sales App main view you'll see the sale you've just added included in the sales list:

	Customer Organisation...	Sale status	Person in charge of sale	Expected value of sale	Probabilit
	Turing's Brain		Thomas Ecclestone	USD 1,000.00	16%

Communications

Communications are phone calls, meetings, letters and so on. It's often important to keep track of what exactly is said during these meetings and Podio provides a simple means to do so.

To open the communications app click 📞 Communic... in the main workspace view. You can add a communication using **+ Add Communication** .

You can add a headline * Headline [   ] which should describe the purpose of the sales call.

Put in who you contacted Add Organisation contact... and based on

72

what lead   Type to search for items   .

Select the type of conversation from the list. Remember that if you use other forms of conversation such as live chat it's possible to   Modify Template   .

Type of communication   Phone call   Email   Online meeting   Met in person

You can specify when the contact happened   Add Date of contact...   and say what happened during the conversation   Add Communication summary...   .

You can also add a file or tags. Save the conversation by clicking on   Save Communication   , print or delete it using   Actions   , add a new conversation using   New Communication   , or return to the communications app by clicking communications from the navigation links   Sales Management > Communications > Talked to turing's brain about new book   .

You'll see the new communication you added on the list of communications and be able to select it and delete it as normal.

Sales Meetings

We've already worked with a meeting app in the Product Management chapter. Sales Meetings are very similar but also include information on Leads, purpose of the meeting and other fields that are of use in a sales content.

To go to the sales app click   Sales Meeti...   in the main workspace view. Click on   + Add Meeting   to add a sales meeting.

First enter a

title   * Meeting Title   Meeting with Turing's Brain editors| .

Then the purpose of the meeting

Qualify lead   Discuss terms of sale   Closing sale   Customer follow-up

Remember that you can   Modify Template   if you want to add other purposes to the meeting.

You can specify the date of the meeting   Add Date of meeting...   and also specify the lead or who the customer is   Type to search for items   ..

In addition to specifying the lead you can say who will/has attended the meeting   Add / Remove participants   .

You can say where the meeting will take place   Add Venue address...   too.

Finally, you can give the meeting an agenda   Add Agenda...   and write the meeting minutes   Add Meeting minutes...   ..

Like all apps you can add tags and files to the meeting.

Once you're happy with the meeting you can save it   Save Meeting ⌄   Delete or print the meeting using   Actions ⌄   , add a new meeting using   New Meeting   or go back to the main sales meeting view by clicking sales meeting in the navigation links.

Sales Management > 🏢 Sales Meetings > Meeting with Turing's Brain editors

When you return to the main sales meeting app view your new sales meeting will be in the list.

Next Chapter

In this Chapter I've described a basic Sales Management platform that can be implemented through standard Podio packs and apps.

I've also shown you how you can customise apps to an extent.

However, Podio provides some much more powerful features that allow you to create entire new apps that mirror your work flow very precisely. The next chapter will show some of this functionality.

4 THE APP BUILDER

So far while we've worked on the sales and lead management workspace we've used apps packages and existing apps. For most purposes this works very well. Podio has a wide range of apps already created for all kinds of purposes.

But as your use Podio more and more sooner or later you end up with a problem.

Podio's premade apps are very good but they won't exactly match your requirements. I've already described one thing you can do to change the apps – you can use modify template to delete, add or modify fields in any app.

But sometimes that isn't enough. Sometimes you need to create an app entirely from scratch. Fortunately, it isn't hard to do this in Podio.

While there is a contracts app in Podio I'm going to show you how to create a very simple contracts app in this section. This is so you'll have the basics of how to add a new app when and if you need it.

The first step to creating a new app is to click ADD APP in the main workspace view.

You'll see an add app dialogue. As a rule I suggest trying to get

an app from the app market Go to the App Market before you create a

new app since this is generally the fastest process.

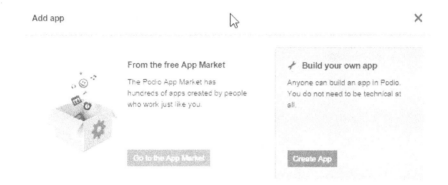

However, for this chapter we're going to create a new app, so

click Create App .

The first stage is to create an app name

App Name *

Contract

It's important that the App name shouldn't be one that you've already included in the workspace.

The next step is to choose an item name. For a sales meeting this might be meeting, for a product app it might be product, in this case I'll call it contract.

Remember, we're dealing with apps – i.e. product, or contract, and items which are just instances of an app. When we added USE Podio in the Product app we were creating a new item.

The next step is to choose an app icons by clicking on the down

App Icon

arrow   .

You'll see a lot of different icons to choose from:

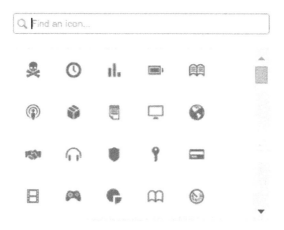

You can scroll down until you see one that you like, in this case I

App Icon

chose the scales: .

It's easy to choose what kind of app view you want by clicking

Default App View

on the down arrow   .

You'll see a list of views:

Click on the one that you want. I suggest ⦀ Table .

Scroll down and enter in a description for the app:

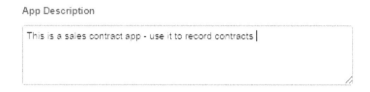

Leave the instructions blanks.

I also suggest leaving the App Types option at the default standard type for now:

App Type

◉ Standard - the Podio default, useful for all types of apps
○ Event - enables RSVP, event notifications and online meeting tools

Once you're happy with your choices, click Create App .

You'll see that you're in a view that looks very similar to the Modify Template view.

On the left of the screen you'll see a list of fields:

Fields

A   Text

☰   Category

📅   Date

👥   Relationship

On the right you'll see a single blank field:

A ·   Title

The first thing to do is click on title (Title   ) in the blank field. You've seen this headline field a number of times, for example in the Lead app it was called Lead, and in the Communications app it was called Headline.

For our app I've chosen to call it Contract Name.

A ·   Contract Name

Congratulations, you've made just about the simplest App it's possible to make!

But it's not much use. You can drag fields across by left clicking and moving them anywhere after the app item name (i.e. anywhere after the first field).

For example, if you want to add a contract status you'd click and hold   ☰   Category   then drag it across to the list of fields:

A　　　　　Contract Name

≡　Category ✥

Then you'd let go:

A　·　　　Contract Name

≡　·　　　Category　　Enter a category option

Go to the underlined section with the field name

≡　·　　　　Category　　and change it to whatever you want the name of the field to be:

≡　·　　　　Contract Status

Like before you'd add the relevant categories by entering them into the box

Enter a category option

For example:

Draft ▾

Live Contact ▾

Obsolete Contract ▾

A Text

Drag and drop a 　　　　　　field, change the

name to Contract Text by editing the field

name **A** ▾　　　　Text .

A ▾　Contract Name

≡ ▾　Contract Status　　Draft

Live Contact

Obsolete Contract

Enter a category option

A ▾　Contract Text

Text　**A**　Text

We've seen a text field in every app so far. You can enter either a line or multiple lines of text into a text field. An example is our first field

Contract Name　|

If you want, you can change some of the properties of the field by clicking the down arrow **A** ▾.

This produces a list of options:

Clicking on an option will activated it. A toggled field will be shown with a tick by it, for example . You can click it again to turn it off.

Required Field is a field that someone must enter before they can save the Item. It's very common for the first (item name) field to be a required field. But any field that you **must** have should be a required field.

Hidden if Empty can only be toggled on if a field isn't a required field. The field will be hidden until you've put data into it. We've seen hidden fields all over the place. They're the ones with greyed out text like .

Single Line means the field will only allow you to enter one line.

Multi Line means the field will allow you to enter multiple lines of text:

Add Help Text brings up the Help text dialogue:

When you start entering information into a field, Podio displays the help text you enter into the dialogue in a little speech bubble to explain the purpose of the field.

Most of these properties are present in each of the following fields. Where there is a new property I will explain it.

Category

We've already seen that to add a new category you type it into the following box:

And to delete a category you hover the mouse over it until the cross appears and then click the cross

You can change the colour of the category by clicking on the

square 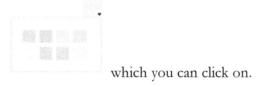 which displays a selection of colours

which you can click on.

When you click on the down arrow to reveal category

properties you'll see that there are number of new ones
compared to the text field:

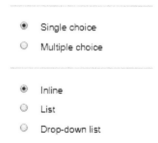

Single Choice means that you can only chose one item at a
time.

Multiple Choice means that you can select more than one item
in the category at once.

Note that in the above example it really only makes sense to
have a single choice field, but there are other fields like book editions

where multiple categories might make sense. A book could be published in eBook, paperback and hardback all at the same time, or in only one format.

Inline list is a category like the one we saw in the above example.

List displays items one after another like the following:

Contract Status

Draft

Live Contact

Obsolete Contract

Drop-Down List is only available for single choice categories. It gives you a combo box

Contract Status | Live Contact ▼ |

Date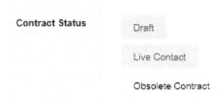

We've seen date fields regularly so far in the book. It's easy to add a new date field. Dates have several additional properties you can access via clicking on the down arrow .

Show in Calendars

If this option is toggled on then anyone who's marked as a calendar will get this item added to their personal calendar. For example, in the sales meetings app above the sales meeting date had a show in calendars field so that the meeting appeared in the personal calendar of anyone who was included in the meeting.

This option also means that the meeting will be displayed in the workspace calendar.

Show Time Entry This will make Podio display the time fields as well as the date field when you're entering the date.

Hide Time Entry This prevents Podio from displaying the time fields when you're entering the date.

Require Time Entry This forces you to enter a time. If you fail to enter a time you won't be able to save the item.

Show End Date So far most of the date fields we've entered are ranges. That's the default scenario, so Podio allows you to enter a beginning and end date.

Hide End Date Prevents you entering an end date, instead you can only enter one day rather than a range of days:

❶	September 2014				❶	
Su	Mo	Tu	We	Th	Fr	Sa
	1	2	3	4	5	6
7	8	9	10	11	12	13
14	15	16	17	18	19	20
21	22	23	24	25	26	27
28	29	30				

Require End Date not only shows an end date but forces you to use it. Until you enter the end date you won't be able to save the item you're creating.

Contact

We've seen contact fields in action, for example in the Product App where Product Owner is a contact field. It's a field that allows you to specify people in the workspace that can be given jobs or own a particular task.

Contact Types / Sharing allows you to control who can be added to this field.

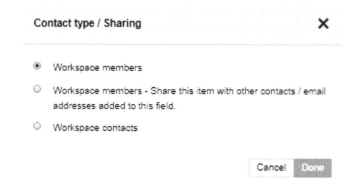

Workspace members restricts the field to those persons who have been invited and opted to join the workspace.

Workspace members – share this item with other contacts / email addresses added to this field will give automatic access to the app to workspace members but will also automatically invited as guests to the item. I.e. people from outside your team will be able to view the item as guests.

Workspace contacts allows anyone to be tagged in the field not just workspace members. Anyone you add to the field will be invited to the item as a guest.

The latter two options are both very useful when making meeting apps, or similar, where you want people from outside the organisation to be able to see the item.

Number

123   Number

A number field allows you to enter a number into a Podio app.

Max Number Of Licenses   55

It prevents you entering special characters such as letters or punctuation (other than decimal places)

Max Number Of Licenses   ab|

Only numbers are allowed

Neither can you add a calculation to the field.

Max Number Of Licenses   5 + 3 =

Only numbers are allowed

When you click on the down arrow to see numbers options *123* you'll find that you can specify

● Display whole number 1,000   Which will display only numbers before the decimal part (whole numbers) so if you were to enter 5.21 it would only display 5.

○ Display two decimals 1,000.50   Displays the number to two decimal points: 5.432 would be displayed at 5.43

○ Display four decimals 1,000.2500   Displays the number to four decimal points.

Image

Image

We've seen an image field before. It allows you to add a picture to your Podio app, for example a photograph of an employee, an advertising image, or a photograph of a building in a property app.

Picture   Add image

Note that you can drag and drop an image from a folder on your

computer to the   Add image   box to add the image.

First, left click and hold the mouse button down on your picture, move your mouse to Podio window

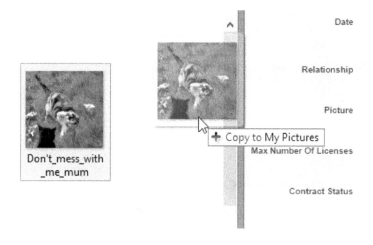

Move the ghost image at the mouse to the   Add image   box

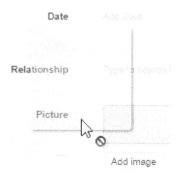

Let go

You may find that it takes Podio a little while before it can upload the picture.

Money Money

We've already seen a money field in action, for example in the Sales app. If you click on the down arrow next to the currency icon you'll find an Set currency... option.

So far we've only been able to add money figures in dollars, but there are Podio users all over the world.

Clicking on Set currency... brings up a currency dialogue

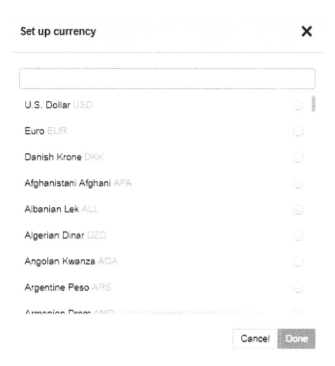

Scroll down to each currency you want to use, and click on it. You'll notice that the square box to the right will be ticked:

Click on it again to toggle it off. You can select as many currencies as you like, then click ▨ when you're happy with it.

Note that when you enter a currency the symbol of the currency that you're currently entering will be displayed:

If you want to add another currency, click on the symbol and a list of the currencies that the field will allow you to enter will be displayed:

Click on the one that you want to enter.

Progress

A progress field is one we've also seen pretty regularly. It produces a scrollbar that shows the percentage completed of a task, or the likelihood of an outcome.

Map

We've seen a map field in the past. Typing a zip code or post code will search for a location:

Clicking on one of the options displays the map

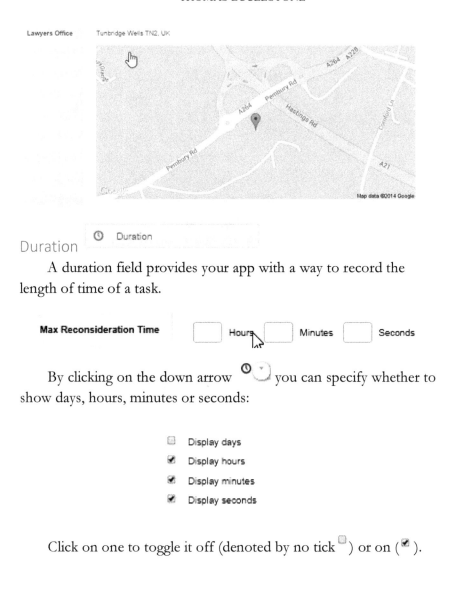

Duration

A duration field provides your app with a way to record the length of time of a task.

By clicking on the down arrow you can specify whether to show days, hours, minutes or seconds:

Click on one to toggle it off (denoted by no tick) or on ( ).

Calculation

A calculation field is not like the other fields we've seen so far that are static fields. It is a dynamic field which changes depending on the data you've entered so far. So, say we have two fields maximum work time, and cost per hour and we wanted a field called maximum cost. We could create a calculation field with the calculation Maximum work time * cost per hour.

Note that you can use the normal mathematical operations addition +, multiplication *, subtraction -, division /, precedence ( ).

So, (a * b) – 3 would result in multiplying a and b together then subtracting 3.

The real strength of the calculation field occurs when you type in @ into the field box.

This produces a list of all the fields in the application. Clicking on one will add the field to the calculation:

You can do multiply, subtract etc. several fields in your app at the same time:

Note that it's also possible to use fields from other apps using the relationships field described below.

If your field calculation results in a number you'll be able to set decimal place options by clicking the down arrow ⬛ ⌄. You'll also be able to Set unit... [.

Set unit   ✕

_____

| Set unit |

                                          Cancel Done

Typing in a unit will add the unit name to the field.

Calculation   10.00 CM

One thing I haven't mentioned so far is that the result of a calculation field can either be a number or text. So, you can combine two pieces of text together by using + (i.e. Name + "working at "+ Organisation might result in "Thomas working at Turing's Brain"), or convert a number field to text. If you have a text item in a field Podio will assume you mean the field to be a text field.

Once Podio has determined what field type the calculation is it won't change. So, if it thinks you're using a number field and you try to change it to concatenate the number to some text Podio won't like it.

If you need to change the calculation type you'll need to delete the field and add it back.

Link 🔗 Link

A link field allows you to include a hyperlink (i.e. a link to a web address).

Hyperlink | Type or paste web address

Once you enter the web address the link is displayed.

Relationships

Although you can obviously only use one app at a time some acts are related to other apps. For example, a Sale is linked to a Lead. This allows the linked app access to fields that it needs in order to do its job.

Adding a relationship field allows you to reference other apps.

So, for example, say you want to reference the contract you used for a sale in the Sales app. In the sales app Modify Template . Add the relationship field as normal.

A app selection dialogue will be displayed.

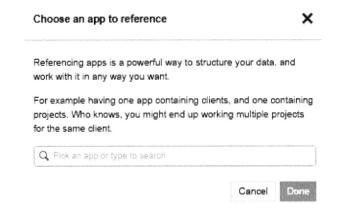

When you click in 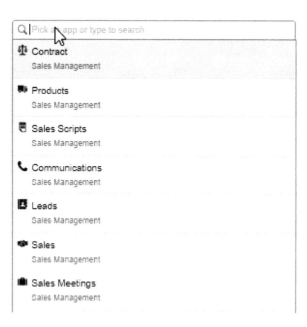 you'll see a list of apps.

Select the apps you want to reference

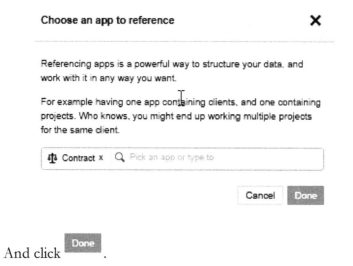

And click Done.

In the actual app you'll see a field like:

Contract   Type to search for items

When you click Type to search for items, you'll see a list of contract's you've entered (in this case, or whatever app you've related the field to)

Note that when you link an app to another app you can access any of the linked apps numerical fields in a calculation field.

When you click the down arrow to reveal relationship properties you see an option Choose an app .

Which brings up the app selection dialogue again.

Note for developers

While it's outside the scope of this book developers may be interested to note that it's possible to use JavaScript in calculation fields in order to increase the dynamic nature of some apps.

Next chapter

In this chapter I've described the app builder and methods of customising Podio to match your business workflow.

The next chapter will introduce apps for a business intranet.

5 A COMPANY INTRANET

With Podio it's easy to make a company intranet which can be used to record company information like vacations, expenses, staff directory, procedures and similar information that people in your company may need to carry out their jobs.

First, click ▤ at the top left hand corner of the screen and click

✛ Create a workspace . Give the new workspace an appropriate name

What do you want to call your workspace?

Company Intranet

Don't forget to set the correct permissions, and click on

Create & Invite

You'll see an invitation dialogue – the same one you saw in chapter three – invite the people you want to join the workspace initially.

You'll end up with an empty workspace.

Click on 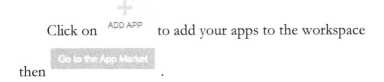 to add your apps to the workspace
then .

In the list of functional areas on the left

click Intranet . You'll see a number of packs
related to company intranets appear on the right:

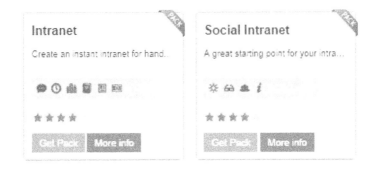

Search for Intranet below:

And click .

The Install pack dialogue will be displayed:

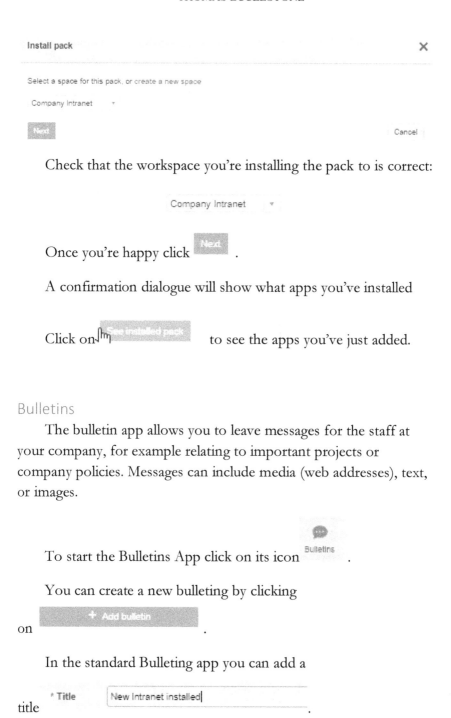

Check that the workspace you're installing the pack to is correct:

Once you're happy click   .

A confirmation dialogue will show what apps you've installed

Click on   to see the apps you've just added.

Bulletins

The bulletin app allows you to leave messages for the staff at your company, for example relating to important projects or company policies. Messages can include media (web addresses), text, or images.

To start the Bulletins App click on its icon   .

You can create a new bulleting by clicking on   .

In the standard Bulleting app you can add a title   .

Clicking on Add Bulletin text.. allows you to add a message to the app.

You can add a web address by clicking on Type or paste web address in the media field.

Or drag and drop an image to the Add image field.

I often adapt the bulleting app by clicking on Modify Template and adding a priority field and urgent attention field:

First drag and drop a ☺ Contact onto the template, and change its name:

☺ Urgent Attention

Click on the down arrow to change the properties ☺ and then Contact types / sharing .

I'd suggest toggling on the ☺ Workspace contacts field in this case. Then click Done ..

Doing this will mean that although any workspace member will be able to see the Bulletins you post, it will be possible to inform specific people that a new bulletin has been posted when it's very important for them to be made aware of it.

To add a priority field drag and drop ☰ Category into the list of fields.

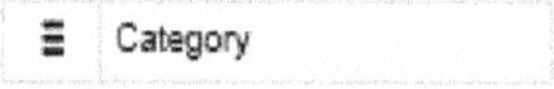

Change the name ☰ ˅ ——————— Priority| and add your relevant priority levels using the

Enter a category option

box.

Clicking the square ˅ will allow you to select different colours for each category:

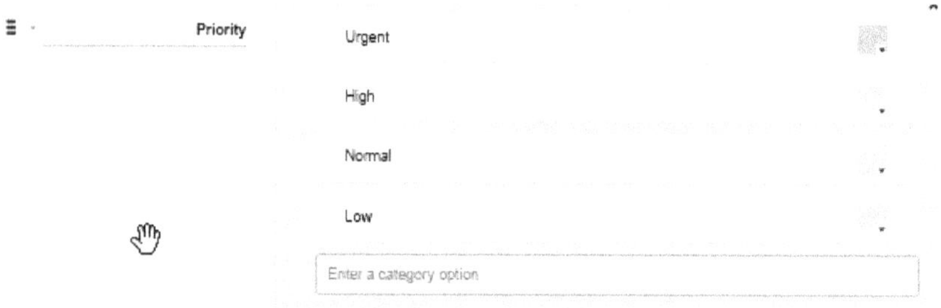

☰ ˅ ———— Priority

Urgent

High

Normal

Low

🖐

Enter a category option

Click **Done** when happy:

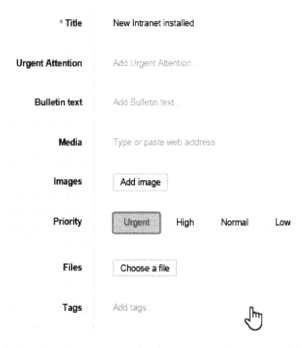

Obviously these customisations are only some of the ones that you might choose for the app, but they are a good start.

You can delete and print from the actions button, or move back to the bulletins app using the navigation link

Company Intranet > 🍥 Bulletins > New Intranet installed to see the list of current bulletins:

Adding a Tile to the Main Workspace View

Here's the thing: the bulleting app isn't all that useful at the moment because you can only see the bulletins when you go into the bulletin app. So, in order to improve matters you might want to add the bulletins to the main workspace view.

Click on 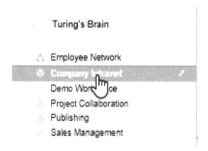 at the top left hand corner of the screen and select your workspace.

Turing's Brain

Employee Network
Company Intranet
Demo Workspace
Project Collaboration
Publishing
Sales Management

You'll see the main workspace view. Click

+ ADD TILE

on

The Workspace Tile Dialogue will be displayed. The default is the overview page which allows you to add calendars, tasks, files, or text or images etc.

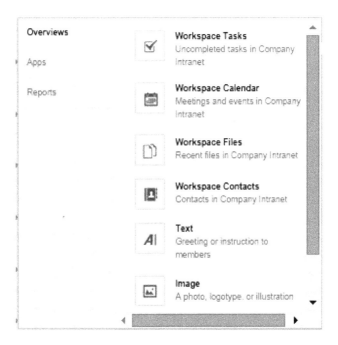

You need to click on Apps which will display a list of apps:

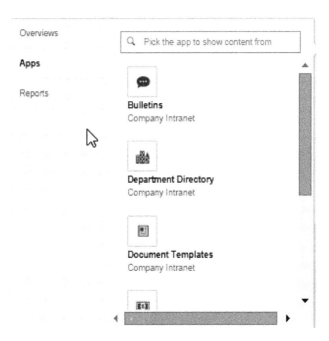

Click on **Bulletins** Company Intranet which will create a bulletin tile:

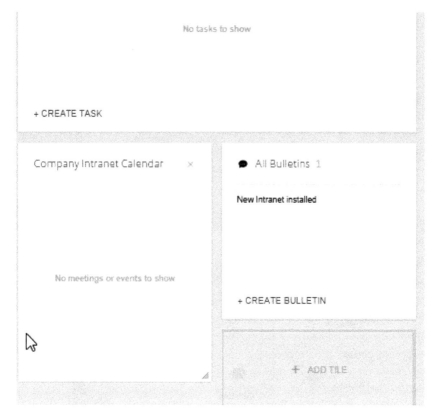

Click and hold the left mouse button on the tile and move it up or down to position it where you want it.

Vacations

When you run a company it's very important to manage vacations effectively to make sure that crucial team functions are running effectively throughout the year.

The Vacations app in Podio provides a simple means of managing vacations effectively.

Click on ❋ to run the app. When you open the app you'll see that it opens in an unusual view – it opens as a calendar which will allow you to see when people are taking vacations.

You can add a vacation by clicking on   **+ Add vacation**   .

When adding a vacation you first enter the name of the person taking the vacation

Then any details about the vacation, for example the purpose of it (if you are taking vacation to look after your family etc.). **Details** Add Details...

Click on Add When are you not available?... to bring up a calendar field to allow you to set the dates of the vacation

When are you not available? | Date 🗓 | HH:MM | — | Date 🗓 | HH:MM |

| ❶ | **September 2014** | | | | ❶ |
Su	Mo	Tu	We	Th	Fr	Sa
	1	2	3	4	5	6
7	8	9	10	11	12	13
14	15	16	17	18	19	20
21	22	23	24	25	26	27
28	29	30				

Click on `Add Who should authorise?...` to bring up a list of workspace members and select one to authorise the vacation.

The final field is `* Authorised?  No  Yes` which can be used to authorise the vacation leave.

You can `Save vacation ⌄` to save the information you've just entered, then create a `New vacation` or go back to the vacations app where you'll see the vacation `Company Intranet ⟩ ✳ Vacations ⟩ Thomas Ecclestone` you've just added.

Sun	Mon	Tue	Wed	Thu	Fri	Sat
				Thomas Ecclestone		
Thomas Ecclestone						

I often do add a pending category to the authorised field:

First, click `Modify Template`. Then add Pending into the Enter a category option box:

≡ ·   Authorised?   No

                                   Yes

                                   Pending| I

Press enter and then move the mouse just to the left of "Pending" and when it changes to a cross arrow click and hold the mouse down and drag it up to the first item on the list then let go.

Pending   ✕

Click the   ▾ to select a new colour for the box:

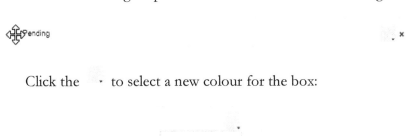

Expenses

All organisations need to control expenses. Naturally, Podio has an app for that.

Click Expenses to start the expenses app.

Then click **+ Add expense** to add an expense.

First, add a short description of the expense by clicking Add Purchase… .

Then Add Date of purchase… .

Use Add Who has bought it?… to put in the name of the person who is to be repaid for the expense.

You can change the status of the

expense Submitted   Approved   Rejected   Reimbursement paid   and also

specify the vendor Add Vendor... and purpose Add Purpose... .

Finally scan, then drag and drop a picture of the receipt

using Add image .

You can save the expense using Save expense ✓ .

While this is a pretty good app it does suffer from the fact that anyone can authorise an expense without there being enough control over the expense process.

Adding an Expense Authorisor App

From the main workspace view click ✛ ADD APP then Create App .

Create New App

General

Advanced

App Name *

Expense Authorisor

Item Name *

Expense Authorisor

App Icon

🔑 ⌄

Default App View

▦ Badge ⌄

App Description

Click on Advanced .

You see a lot of options in this advanced view. You can stop Podio automatically displaying new items in the app in the activity stream, or just edits to the app in the stream:

☐ Do not post new items to stream

☐ Do not post item edits to stream

You can also stop members receiving emails when they are added to a contact field in the app

☐ Disable notifications for items created / edited / deleted for users that follow this app

But what we're interested in is stopping anyone who is just a workspace member adding items to the app. Toggle these two fields on:

☑ Don't let members add items to this app

☑ Don't let members edit items in this app

This will prevent anyone who doesn't have administrative access entering data into the app.

You can also ☐ Show unique ID or ☐ Disable comments . When you're happy click Create App

This will bring up the App builder.

Change the first field so it's called
A ˅ _____ Role
Role , and select the properties **A** ˅ .

Make it a required field by toggling ☑ Required field .

Drag and drop a 👤 Contact field into the app. Change the name to Role Holder:

113

Then select the properties .

Make it a required field by toggling ☑ Required field .

Then select Done .

An administrator can add an expense authorisor by clicking

✦ Add Expense Authorisor in the Expense A... app.

* Role	manager
Role Holder	Thomas Ecclestone
	Add/Remove

Saving it using Save Expense Authorisor ˅ . If you want you can add tips in the way described in the last chapter.

Linking Expenses to Expense Authorisor App

Go into the company intranet workspace by clicking it in the navigation links Company Intranet ♀ Expense Authorisor › Manager .

Open the expenses app by clicking on its icon Expenses .Then click on the spanner icon on the right hand side

Click on  from the list of options:

Drag a  field into the list of fields. Rename it authorisor:

Then select the properties and toggle on.

This will force anyone adding an expense claim to reference one of the people in the organisation who are respobsible for authorising claims when the record is created. Click on Done when you are happy with the app that you've just edited.

Managing Workflows

Sometimes you may want something like a notification to happen when you update or create a new item. You can use the managing workflows feature in Podio to do this.

Click the spanner in your app and ℕ Manage workflows .

You'll see the workflow window:

Workflows for Expenses

Create workflow

Workflow automate processes on Podio, so you don't have to do the clicking. They can be simple or powerful, and take minutes to setup.

Give it a try.

Create Workflow

Click Create Workflow .

The first step is to choose when the workflow will be activated.

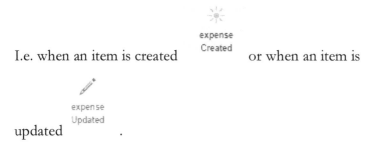

I.e. when an item is created expense Created or when an item is updated expense Updated .

In this example we're going to use the default Expense Created setting.

The second step is chose to add a task   or a

comment   drag the option you want onto the

Drag in an effect from above box. In this case, I'm going to add a task.

Title   Please Authorize expense

Give the task a descriptive title

The next stage is to choose who to assign the item

Assign to   Q Type to search or click to add

to. ————————————————. You can either choose to assign it to a specific workspace member or to a variable. A variable is one of the contact fields in the app.

Variables

Created by

Who has bought it?

Authorisor

Current user or app

In this case I'm going to assign the task to the Authorisor.

Assign to   Authorisor x

You can also set a due date

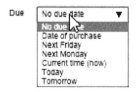

The due date can be the a variable in the app (i.e. Date of purchase) or a date based on the time when the workflow is triggered (i.e. the next day (tomorrow).)

Finally, you can enter in details

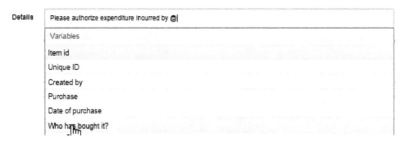

When entering in details don't forget that you can use the @ operator to enter in variables from the app.

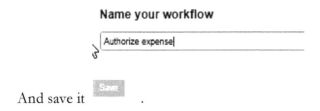

You've created your task.

The final step is to name the workflow

Name your workflow

And save it  .

You'll return to the workflow view, where you'll see a list of current workflows

To open a workflow for editing click on it in the list

Existing workflows

Authorize expense

To delete a workflow click on the 🗑 by its name:

Authorize expense   🗑

Return to the app by clicking its icon (e.g. for expenses Expenses .

The effect of the above changes are that the Responsible Person will be automatically get a task to authorize the expense. They'll see it in their task list, and if they've set their notifications up correctly will receive it by email.

Department Directory

Every good intranet has a Department Directory where you can find contacts in different Departments in your organisation.

Click on Department in the main workspace view to open up the department directory. Then Add department to add a department.

First, enter the name of the department

* Department Name |

Then select a head of department Add Head of department... , and any staff you want Add Staff....

You can describe the business area using Add Function... and give the department a location using Add Location... .

Save the department by clicking Save department ∨ .

Exporting information from an App into Excel

Sometimes you may want to export information from Podio into a spreadsheet. This is easy to do. Click the spanner at the top right hand corner of the screen in the main app view

From the list of options click on 🔁 Excel Export .

You'll see information describing the progress of the export and saying when the export is complete on the bottom left hand of the screen

Click on the notification that the export is complete:

You'll be taken to the export app screen. Click on the file link:

The file will download as normal. You can save it to a new location, or open it, in the same way you always do on your browser:

When you open the excel file you'll notice that it contains hidden fields such as created on, created by, which Podio stores as a way of maintaining an audit trail. The spreadsheet file also includes information stored in apps referenced in contact fields and sometimes related apps.

The ability to export files into spreadsheets can be very useful since it allows you to integrate the app into your other systems, backup your apps and migrate to other systems if necessary.

Importing information from Excel into an App

It is possible to import information from excel into an app. Because this is a beginners guide importing information from excel is beyond the books scope because it can be risky. You can, however, find information on how to do it at https://help.podio.com/hc/en-us/articles/201019618-Importing-from-Excel

Procedures

The procedures app is a file store that you can use to maintain an intranet of current operating rules and methodology for your organisation.

You can access the procedures app by clicking Procedures in the main workspace view, and add a new procedure by

clicking + Add procedure .

First you can add a title that describes the procedure,

* Title |

Then a full description of the procedure Add Description... .

Then you can put in the owner of the procedure Add Responsible person... and drag and drop the procedure on to

Choose a file .

Clone an App before editing it

While you are developing apps you may sometimes want to work on a dummy app to work out exactly what changes you want to make.

You can copy an app by using the clone functionality.

Click on the spanner at the top right hand corner of the app

view ✈ .

Click on ⊘ Clone app   from the list.

You'll see a clone dialogue where you can choose the workspace the new app will be cloned to:

Choose the space you'd like to clone your app into:

Company Intranet   ·

And also be able to choose whether to clone the content of the app:

☐ Also clone the contents of the app.

Often you'll have two workspaces – a production workspace and a development workspace. Using the clone facility you'll copy a development app into the production workspace, export data from the exiting app and import it into the new app.

Naturally, only an administrator can clone an app.

Archiving an App

Archiving an app means that all the existing information in it remains, but you can't add or change the data in the app.

To Archive an App click on the spanner at the top right hand

side of the main app view ✈ then click on ⊘ Archive app . You'll see a confirmation dialogue appear:

Disable app

Are you sure you wish to disable Procedures?

Yes   No

Click yes.

Delete an App

It's possible to delete an App, but not recommended. This will permanently remove your App from your workspace. You won't be able to change your mind later on.

To delete an App click on the spanner at the top right hand side of the main app view ✦ then click on 🗑 Delete app you'll see a confirmation dialogue appear:

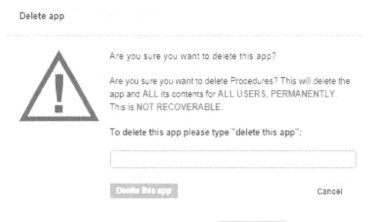

Type in the text it wants and then Delete this app .

Document Templates

A document template is a document that you can modify for specific purposes, such as a sales letter of invoice. Podio provides a simple Document Templates app that you can access by clicking on Document... . You can create a new Document Template by clicking on + Add template .

First enter your document templates

* Title

name and a description of the document template Add Description... .

You can specify conditions on when to use the template

Internally Externally Both externally and internally

And also whether the template is in use or not:

Draft In use - live No longer in use - archived

Each document has a person who is responsible for making sure that it is up to date or not

Add Responsible for updating... .

Drag and drop the template onto Choose a file . Once you're happy click Save template .

Email to App

It's possible to email an app so that the email is added to the app. This can be very useful when integrating bespoke software into Podio, or dealing with emails that are used by people who are not members of Podio yet.

While how to do this is beyond a beginner's guide you can find out more about this functionality at https://help.podio.com/hc/en-us/articles/201019648-Email-to-app

Staff Meetings

We've already seen several meetings apps. The intranet allows you to set up staff meetings, as supposed to (e.g.) Project or Sales meetings. It's pretty self-explanatory at this point.

To run the meeting app click on . You can create a staff meeting by clicking on

+ Add staff meeting

.

Give the meeting a title, Title

Add a time Meeting date and time   Add Meeting date and time...

Say who you want to attend the meeting Add / Remove participants .
And add the agenda, minutes, and Location for the meeting

Agenda   Add Agenda...

Minutes   Add Minutes...

Location   Add Location...

Then save the meeting using Save staff meeting . You can add a new meeting, print, delete or navigate to the staff meeting app in the normal way.

Next Chapter

In this chapter I've described how to build a company intranet using Podio. I've also gone into a lot more detail about how to modify apps, restrict who can update them, manage workflows and maintain apps.

In the next chapter I'll describe some more features of Podio that aid communication between staff members.

6 REPORTS, TASKS AND COMMUNICATIONS

This chapter will show how to use Podio to increase communications within your organisation. You can use Podio's report functionality to summarise the information you have available in your Podio apps, can comment within apps, manage tasks and communicated within your team using the chat functionality within Podio.

Reports

To make a report click on ~~Actions~~ and select ^{Make a report} .

You'll see the Report window

Function		Select a field or enter a number	Select operator	Select a field or enter a number	x
Count	▾	of None	None	None	=

The first step is to choose a function Count ▾ :

Count specifies the number of items in the view

Sum which adds all the items in a field together

Average gives you a medium average of all the numbers in the

127

field

Minimum gives you the lowest value in the field

Maximum gives you the highest value in the field

Where you are using a function that requires a number (i.e. Sum, average, minimum, maximum) you can select the field that you want the function to operate on.

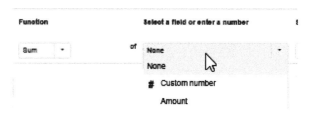

For example

Would give you the highest number in the amount field (i.e. the report would show the highest amount).

The result of the function is displayed on the right hand of the screen:

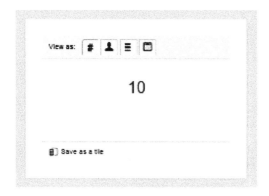

This function can be useful for showing the number of results of a particular report, or maximum or minimum of a number field etc. What it can't do is show you a list of items that match a particular description. To do this we need to use the filtering options.

First click to change the layout of the report. There are several options:

You're currently in Badge, which shows you information with items in a rectangular box. Click on table which lists information in a table:

Click on 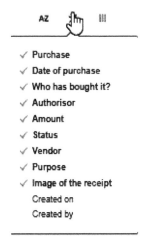 which brings up a list of table fields:

You can deselect or select fields by clicking on them. Say, you only want to see Purchase, Who has bought it, Status and amount. Click on all the other fields with ticks by them.

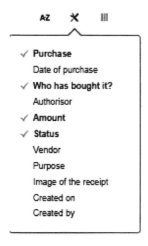

Will produce a table similar to:

	‹ Purchase	Who has bought it?	Amount	Status
1	LibreOffice Writer Help		USD 2,000.00	Approved
2	Celestia Book		USD 12.00	Approved
3	Bought Book	Thomas Ecclestone	USD 10.00	Approved

We can also control the way fields are sorted by clicking on ^{AZ}. You'll see a list of fields. Depending on whether the field is a date, number, or text you'll see different options. For example you can sort a date by oldest or newest first, or a text field by A-Z or Z-A.

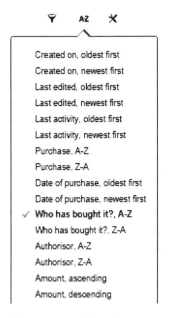

In this case I'm going to sort it by Amount, ascending by clicking on Amount, ascending .

	< Purchase	Who has bought it?	Amount	Status
1	Bought Book	Thomas Ecclestone	USD 10.00	Approved
2	Celestia Book		USD 12.00	Approved
3	LibreOffice Writer Help		USD 2,000.00	Approved

Restricting and sorting the report is a good start, but we can also set conditions on the fields that are shown in the report. Click on the filtering icon ▼ . This will bring up a screen that shows you what filters are already being applied on the right.

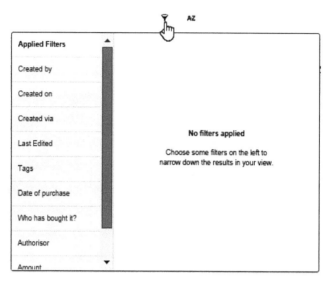

On the left of the screen is a list of fields. Click on the one you want to filter by. In this case I want to show all results less than $100 so I click on Amount.

Because this is a number field you see the filter fields which are based on current entries. Since the largest amount is 2000, and the smallest amount is 10, it is displaying all current expenses:

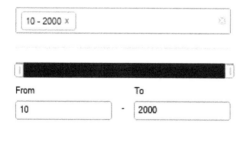

To

100

I change the To field:

And we can see our results filtered so they only show amounts less than $100:

	‹ Purchase	Who has bought it?	Amount	Status
	Bought Book	Thomas Ecclestone	USD 10.00	Approved
2	Celestia Book		USD 12.00	Approved

Podio is intelligent because it customises the filters based on the field type, so a date field will allow you to filter by a custom date range or a variety of options from the past, present and future.

Custom Date	›
All	
Past	
Yesterday	
7 days	
30 days	
Year	

Whereas a contact field can be filtered by whether it is yourself, not yourself, or a particular workspace member. A Category field can be filtered by whether it's been set to a particular category or not set at all.

You can change your mind and remove all the filters by clicking on ᵇʰᵒʷ ᵃˡˡ or a specific filter by clicking on the filters icon

▼ ● then ᴬᵖᵖˡⁱᵉᵈ ᶠⁱˡᵗᵉʳˢ and the little cross by the filter that you want to remove.

Amount	✖ Clear all
10 - 100 ✕	

You can save the results of your report by clicking on Save view .
This will bring a Save View As dialogue. Give the report a reasonable name:

Expenses Less than $100|

And press Save view .

Note that when you are using a report that you've saved and go back to the main app view it will display the last view (in other words the report) that you've just used:

⊙ Expenses Less than $100 2 of 3

Click on the above report name to see a list of all views

Click on the view that you want to use.

Note that you can also save the tile at the right of the screen by clicking ▣ Save as a tile

You will have to enter a title that is descriptive

Enter a title

and then select where you want to save the tile Save this report on... This app's sidebar ▼ you can chose between the apps sidebar, your workspace, employee home or the home page. If you choose home page you'll see it every time you open Podio.

Click Save when you're happy.

You'll see the summary view appear whenever you are on the page you selected (i.e. the app view, or homepage etc):

Managing tasks

We've already seen tasks described in Chapter One, and throughout the book but so far I haven't described how you can manage them. The process is very simple. Click  at the top of the screen to bring up the task manager.

You can see completed tasks by clicking on All completed (i.e. tasks completed by anyone) or My completed tasks to show the tasks that you've completed:

Clicking on My delegated tasks will show you tasks that you've given to someone else:

If there is a line through them they've been completed. If they are red the task is overdue.

Tasks can be assigned automatically in apps through the workflow process that I've described previously. But you can also assign yourself or someone else a task in this window by clicking on My tasks and then clicking on the "enter a task box".

Which will bring up task assignment options

First describe the task ☑ Write book|

Then pick who you want to assign the task to.

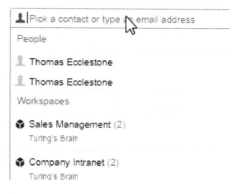

Leaving the box empty means the task will be assigned to you.

You can set a due date and time 🗓 No due date ▾ 🕐 --:-- . If you set these fields to a date in the future you'll be able to set a reminder 🕐 for whoever has the task.

You can also make the task repeat daily, weekly etc. by clicking

on the repeat button

This can be used to remind you of regular tasks.

You can choose what workspace or task to attach the task to, for example sales meeting, or employee network:

Finally, add information about the task, add any tags or files to the task and click . .

You'll see the task you've created in the appropriate list.

Clicking on the next to a task says that you've completed it.

Clicking on the date allows you to change the due date:

☐ 09/11/2014 ▾
☐ No due date
☐ Today
☐ Tomorrow
☐ Next Monday
☐ Custom date

Clicking on the name

☐ 09/11/2014   (Write book)

Will bring up a screen that will allow you to enter information about the task *i* Enter more information about your task ... , add a comment, reassign it by clicking on the ♟ icon or make it private by clicking on the 🔒 icon.

Clicking on My tasks will bring up your list of tasks again.

If you've completed all tasks, it'll display:

You have no outstanding tasks, nice work!

Note that pressing T on any screen in Podio (other than when you're adding information into a field!) will create a new task.

Chat
You can do video conferencing, audio conferencing and text chat using Podio. Find out more at https://help.podio.com/hc/en-us/articles/201020148-Using-Messages-Chat .

Comments
Anywhere in Podio where you can see an Activity Steam there

are also comments available. Click on 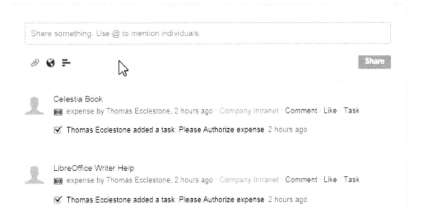 Activity and you'll see the activity stream for the entire workspace:

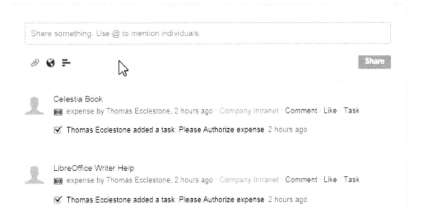

If you type in something into the Share Something box it'll be added to the activity stream. If you use @ it'll bring up a contacts list:

Any contact you mention when sharing will be notified.

Click ⌀ to share a file or ⊕ to share a link. ⚏ marks what you're sharing as a question.

Anyone who has something to say about something on the activity stream can click on Comment

And type whatever they want, remembering they can also use the @ symbol to reference a person.

Then press [Add comment] to add the comment to the steam:

Note that in individual items when editing an item you've already created and saved you see the activity stream on the right, but can also click on comments

Which brings up a list of existing comments on that particular item

And a box that allows you to add more comments

Then click  .

Note that comments will also show up on your personal activity stream which you can access by clicking on your name anywhere in the activity or comments log

When you click it you'll see the comments you've added, items you've edited, tasks you've completed or assigned and anything else that you've done in Podio. You'll be able to add comments too.

Hover your mouse over a comment and then click the delete icon at the top right hand side of the comment 🗑 and you'll delete the comment.

Search

When you click on the 🔍 icon you open up a search box:

Search can be a little difficult to understand since the exact results depend on where you are. The above search box is displaying a general search that you see when you just open up Podio. You also see a list of apps below it:

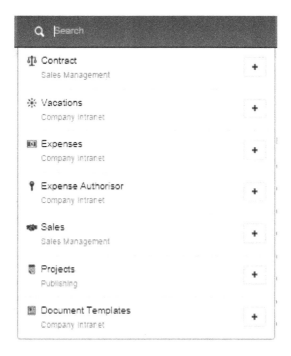

Clicking on the ⁺ symbol will add a new item of that app type.

Typing in a words such as Documents will search all your workspaces with apps of that name:

Clicking on Show all results for: Document > substantially widens the search.

Once you go into a workspace the search narrows to items

within that workspace.

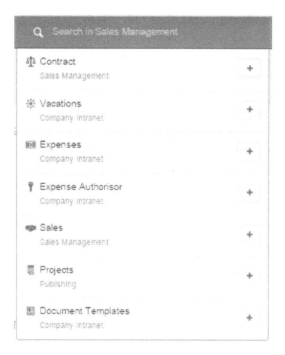

Again, though, it produces a list of apps. Clicking on one of the apps, such as Contract will open the contact main view.

Once you're in an app, a search is more specific still, allowing you to search for specific items:

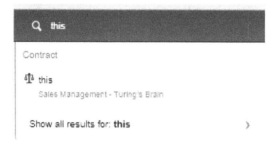

Clicking on the show all results in a search sends you to a results page:

Showing results from "Sales Management" workspace (Search all workspaces)

| 🔍 that | Search |

this and that
👤 Status by Thomas Ecclestone a few seconds ago

Books Sales Script
📖 Sales Script by Thomas Ecclestone 6 days ago

I've just described some of the features of search, but it should be obvious now why apps have labels – a consistent label scheme allows you much faster searching since you can use tags that describe your item and that can be searched for using the feature described above.

Help and Support

Click on ? then Help Center and contact support for more information about Podio, or 💡 General help forum to ask a question.

Viewing Contacts

Click 🖼️ to view contacts . You'll see a list of the current contacts you have.

Type in a contact name into 🔍 Search contacts to search for him or her.

Click on actions by the name to get a list of things that you can do to the contact.

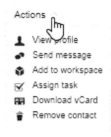

Note that contacts include workspace members but also people you've added in other apps via their email. Where a contact isn't part of Podio you can invite them to join it when appropriate.

Manage Notifications

Click on ![notifications icon] to show your notifications.

Click on Email settings to control what emails Podio sends you.

You can toggle on or off certain types of notification, for example if you don't want to be emailed when changes in membership occurs you'd toggle off

☑ Changes in workspace membership occur (add, leave, join etc)

So long, and thanks

I've really enjoyed working on this book, and it's great that we've got this far together. Although this is a beginners' guide I hope that I've shown you everything you need to get started with Podio. This tool is simple and elegant to use, and I hope it – and this book! – will help your organisation achieve everything it attempts.

If you have any questions don't hesitate to email me, personally, on thomasecclestone@yahoo.co.uk .

And thanks!

ABOUT THE AUTHOR

Thomas Ecclestone is a software engineer and technical writer who lives in Kent, England. After getting his 1st class honours in software engineering he worked at the National Computing Centre in Manchester, the Manchester Metropolitan University, and for BEC systems Integration before starting his own business in software development. He is a writer who lives on a smallholding in Kent where he looks after a small flock of Hebridean sheep.

www.ingramcontent.com/pod-product-compliance
Lightning Source LLC
Chambersburg PA
CBHW071001050326
40689CB00014B/3443